About the Book

Dinosaur Jim Jensen, a scientist, was searching for dinosaur bones on a cliff high above a piney valley in Colorado. Using picks and shovels, he and his helpers carefully dug for buried fossils—bones from ancient dinosaurs, crocodiles, turtles and other creatures.

Then one day Dinosaur Jim found a strange bone. The fossil was so huge that it took two days to dig it out from the greenish-gray clay that covered it. The strange bone turned out to be a hip bone from the most gigantic dinosaur anyone had ever found. Dinosaur Jim dug out more of the dinosaur's bones. From them he learned that his discovery had been a giant among dinosaurs. So he named this huge dinosaur "Supersaurus." One hundred feet long, Supersaurus lived 150 million years ago when the earth was very different.

Here is a true story about one man's remarkable hunt for dinosaur fossils and what they reveal about the ancient past.

A SEE & READ BOOK

SUPERSAURUS

by Francine Jacobs
pictures by D.D. Tyler

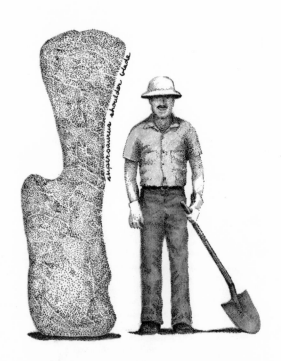

supersaurus shoulder blade

G.P. Putnam's Sons
New York

The author and illustrator wish to thank paleontologist
Michael K. Brett-Surman for his generous assistance.

Text copyright © 1982 by Francine Jacobs.
Illustrations copyright © 1982 by D.D. Tyler.
All rights reserved. Published simultaneously in
Canada by General Publishing Co. Limited, Toronto.
Printed in the United States of America.
Library of Congress Cataloging in Publication Data
Jacobs, Francine.
Supersaurus.
(A See & read book)
Summary: Details a paleontologist's 1972 discovery in
western Colorado of the biggest dinosaur bones yet.
1. Dinosaurs — Juvenile literature. [1. Dinosaurs]
I. Tyler, D. D., ill. II. Title. III. Series: See & read book.
QE862.D5J27   567.9'1   81-7375   AACR2
ISBN 0-399-61150-9
First impression.

For Barbara and Perry Jeffe — F.J.
For Kate's big brother, Zachary — D.D.T.

Dinosaur Jim stared at

the amazing bone

his friends had found.

It was a fossil,

an ancient bone

millions of years old

that had become hard as rock.

The bone was as large as a man's shoe.

Not very big as bones go.

But huge for a toe bone.

Jim could tell from its roundish shape

that the bone had come

from a large

meat-eating dinosaur.

Jim Jensen is a scientist
who knows lots about dinosaurs.
He will go almost anywhere
to look for their bones.
That's why people call him
Dinosaur Jim.
So of course he could hardly wait
to see where his friends
had found this bone.
And off they went.
They drove to a dry, piney valley.

His friends had found the bone,
uncovered, on the valley floor.
But fossil bones are usually
covered with earth.
So Dinosaur Jim looked around
to see where this fossil
could have come from.
He saw a high, flat cliff above him.
"See where the wind and rain
wore the earth away," he said.
"The bone must have fallen from there."
Maybe Dinosaur Jim could find
more of the dinosaur's bones.

So he called his son
and another young man to help him.
They set up camp on the cliff.
And they began to dig.
They dug slowly and carefully
so as not to break anything.

13

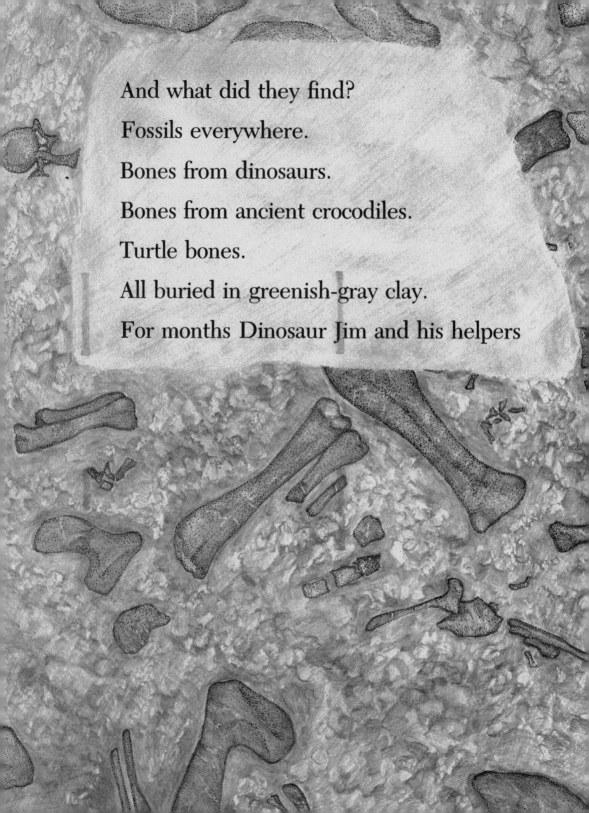

And what did they find?

Fossils everywhere.

Bones from dinosaurs.

Bones from ancient crocodiles.

Turtle bones.

All buried in greenish-gray clay.

For months Dinosaur Jim and his helpers

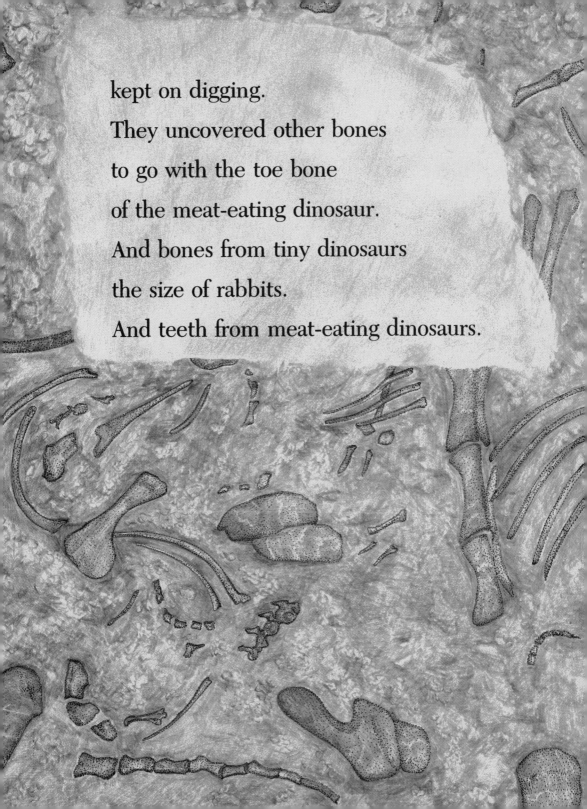

kept on digging.
They uncovered other bones
to go with the toe bone
of the meat-eating dinosaur.
And bones from tiny dinosaurs
the size of rabbits.
And teeth from meat-eating dinosaurs.

Then one day

Dinosaur Jim found something odd.

Big.

Different from anything he'd ever seen.

He worked the clay away all day.

And still it was half-buried.

It was certainly a large fossil.

That night Dinosaur Jim came out
of his tent
and looked at the bone in the moonlight.
The fossil was so big it puzzled him.
Next morning he could hardly wait
to start digging again.
He scraped away the clay
that still covered the fossil.
His curiosity grew and grew
with each bit of bone he uncovered.

Finally, in the afternoon,

he could tell what bone he was uncovering.

It was the hip bone

of a gigantic dinosaur.

The fossil was six feet across.

It was as wide as a car.

Could Dinosaur Jim and his helpers

be on the trail

of the biggest dinosaur ever?

Right away

they grabbed their picks and shovels.

More good luck!

Another huge bone.

Another.

Another.

They found enormous rib, neck,
and shoulder bones.
One of the neck bones was as long as
a teacher's desk.
The shoulder bones were so long,
eight people could have fit in a line
on each of them.
These dinosaur bones were bigger by far
than any ever found before.
This must have been a super dinosaur.
A brand-new discovery.
It didn't even have a name!

News of Dinosaur Jim's find
got around quickly.
It was on the radio.
And television.
It was in the newspapers.
Everyone was talking about it.

People came from 22 states
to see the enormous fossils.
They crowded around the bones
and shook their heads in wonder.

Dinosaur Jim could tell
a lot about the super dinosaur
from the size and shape of its bones.
It had been an adult,

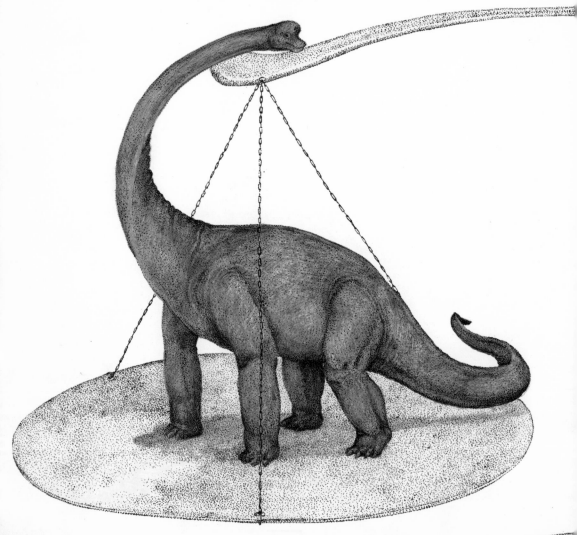

not a young dinosaur.

It must have weighed about 70 tons,

as much as 14 circus elephants

all together.

The super dinosaur had stood
over 50 feet tall,
taller than a five-story building.
And its neck was as long as
a telephone pole.
The dinosaur could stretch about 100 feet
from the tip of its chin
to the end of its tail.
Dinosaur Jim could picture
the huge animal.
It had four giant, elephant-like legs.
And was a plant-eater.
Dinosaur Jim could tell this
because its hip bone
was like that of other large
plant-eating dinosaurs.

The super dinosaur was a gentle giant.
It had moved slowly through
the western part of North America
about 150 million years ago,
long before there were people.

There were only two seasons then.
It was hot and sometimes rainy.
And cool and dry at other times.
The big dinosaur must have
waded in wide rivers.

It must have plodded on dry land,

bumping and crashing

through thick evergreen forests.

Maybe it traveled with similar dinosaurs

in small groups.

Its normal step was about

9 feet long.

And its five-toed feet

left footprints

as large as kitchen sinks.

Of course it took a lot to feed

such a huge body.

Maybe 1300 pounds of plants each day.

So the dinosaur

spent most of its time eating.

It munched on ferns.

It stretched its long neck
to strip the tops
from evergreen trees.
It didn't chew its food,

but gobbled it down whole.

Not that it was in a hurry.

Eating took hours

because it had a small mouth.

And its head was only about three feet long

even though the dinosaur was so big.

In fact, its brain

was only the size of a hen's egg.

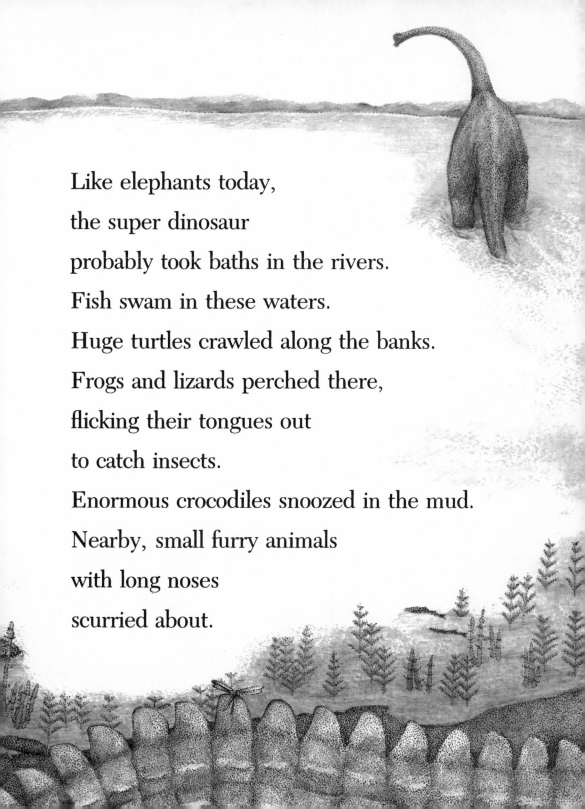

Like elephants today,

the super dinosaur

probably took baths in the rivers.

Fish swam in these waters.

Huge turtles crawled along the banks.

Frogs and lizards perched there,

flicking their tongues out

to catch insects.

Enormous crocodiles snoozed in the mud.

Nearby, small furry animals

with long noses

scurried about.

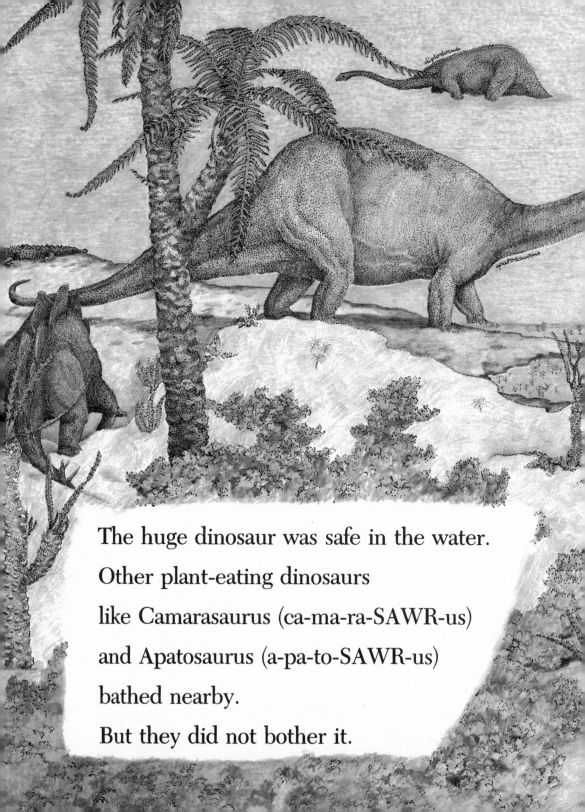

The huge dinosaur was safe in the water.
Other plant-eating dinosaurs
like Camarasaurus (ca-ma-ra-SAWR-us)
and Apatosaurus (a-pa-to-SAWR-us)
bathed nearby.
But they did not bother it.

On land, however,
there were dangers.
Enemies!
Fierce, meat-eating dinosaurs,
like Allosaurus (al-lo-SAWR-us),
hid in the dark forests.

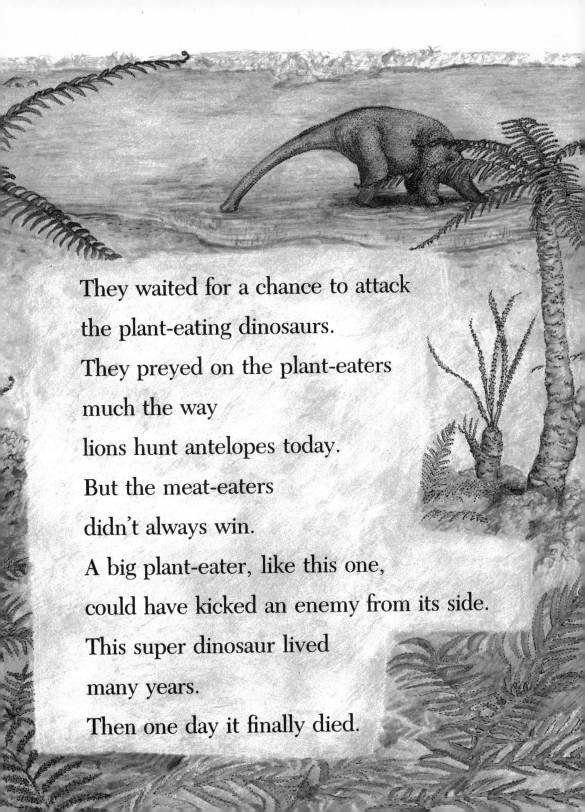

They waited for a chance to attack
the plant-eating dinosaurs.
They preyed on the plant-eaters
much the way
lions hunt antelopes today.
But the meat-eaters
didn't always win.
A big plant-eater, like this one,
could have kicked an enemy from its side.
This super dinosaur lived
many years.
Then one day it finally died.

Meat-eaters probably feasted
on its flesh.
Then flood waters must have
swept its remains
into a river
where it floated downstream
and came to rest
in shallow water.
The huge carcass blocked the stream
and formed a dam.
Other dead animals piled up
around it.
Sand and gravel slowly
buried their bones.
Over thousands of years
minerals from the earth hardened them
into fossils.

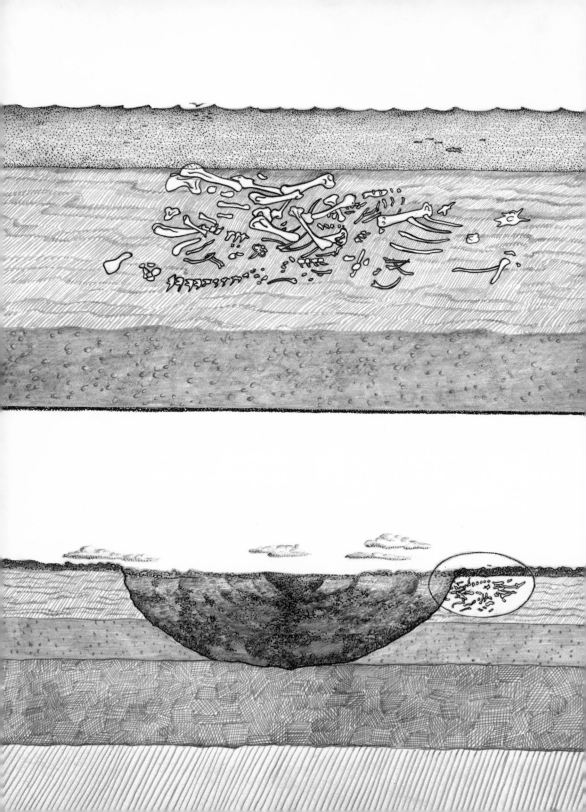

Then shallow seas came
and covered the fossils with clay.
Millions of years went by.
The earth pushed up
to form the high, flat cliff.
And the seas disappeared.
Wind and water slowly wore the
covering earth away.
Then one bone tumbled free,
and Dinosaur Jim came along
to dig the others up.
Now he had to protect them.
He and his crew
painted the fossils with shellac
and covered them with plaster.
Carefully, they hoisted the fossils
onto trucks and took them to a museum.

There are 16 tons of bones
to sort and study.
Which fit?
Which do not?
Dinosaur Jim has a giant puzzle
to put together.
And he's still digging for missing parts.
But he has come up with a name
for his big, new, super dinosaur.
He calls it SUPERSAURUS.
What else?

About Those Bones

SUPERSAURUS is a true story. Dr. James A. Jensen is a field paleontologist (pa-le-on-TOL-o-gist), a scientist who hunts for fossil bones. He is a director of the Earth Sciences Museum at Brigham Young University in Provo, Utah, where he is known as Dinosaur Jim. Dr. Jensen began the search for SUPERSAURUS in the spring of 1972 at a place called Dry Mesa in western Colorado. He continues to dig for fossils there. He hopes one day to assemble the bones and show the skeleton of SUPER-SAURUS. Dr. Jensen believes that SUPERSAURUS looked something like the huge plant-eater Brachiosaurus (brake-e-o-SAWR-us), but was bigger. Other scientists, however, are not agreed on the type of dinosaur he discovered: whether it is a Brachiosaurus or a Diplodocus (dip-LAH-do-cus).

In 1979, Dr. Jensen found another dinosaur's toe bones. He also uncovered a nine-foot shoulder bone that is even larger than that of SUPERSAURUS. For now, he is calling this new discovery ULTRASAURUS.